The Base Strategy:

Simplify, Arrange, and Optimize Your Digital Career

MICHAEL T. BATCHELOR

DISCLAIMER

TABLE OF CONTENT

Contents

INTRODUCTION

SETTING THE FOUNDATION

Opening Quote or Prologue

In the ever-evolving fabric of our digital era, where jobs are formed in the furnace of technology, we find ourselves navigating a maze of opportunities and obstacles. As T.S. Eliot succinctly stated, "Only those who will risk going too far can possibly find out how far one can go." These statements resonate strongly as we go on a quest to discover the deeper techniques of simplicity, organization, and optimization in the digital professional environment.

Prologue: The Digital Odyssey

In a world bursting with information and connection, a key event transpires that parallels the universal struggle of professionals seeking clarity within the digital cacophony. Imagine a figure, representative of every career enthusiast, poised at the intersection of tradition and innovation. A strange invitation arrives, with the enigmatic promise of a transforming approach to the basic strategy. Little does our protagonist know, this is the beginning of a mission that will reshape their digital fate.

Author's Note

Dear Reader, As the inventor of "The Base Strategy," I come before you not just as an author but as a fellow traveler in the domains of digital vocations. My obsession with this subject is more than a professional quest; it's a personal voyage generated from the intersections of ambition, challenge, and the constant pursuit of greatness in the digital era. In the next chapters, we'll study the delicate ballet between simplicity, arrangement, and optimization a dance that may lift your digital career to unequaled heights.

This book is not a mere guidebook; it's a testament to the significant influence that purposeful choices can have on one's career trajectory. Simplifying, organizing, and optimizing are not simply methods; they are the guiding concepts that light the route to success in today's changing digital world. They constitute the base upon which we construct professions that not only endure but flourish among the swift currents of change.

I welcome you to join me on this revolutionary journey. As we go into the core of digital career dynamics, let's unearth the secrets that will enable you to succeed in the ever-shifting landscapes of the professional world. With zeal and effort, [Michael T. Batchelor] Author, "The Base Strategy: Simplify, Arrange, and Optimize Your Digital Career

CHAPTER 1

THE LANDSCAPE OF THE DIGITAL CAREER

Evolving Digital Trends

In the broad expanse of the digital frontier, change is not just constant; it's speeding. As we continue our investigation of the digital career environment, it's vital to grasp the forces moving us ahead.

Remote Work: Redefining

Boundaries

The rise of remote work has become a

characteristic of the digital era. Explore

how this movement has demolished

geographical constraints, allowing professionals to participate in global efforts without leaving the comfort of their homes. Delve into the consequences for work-life balance, cooperation, and the shifting nature of teamwork.

Artificial Intelligence:

Navigating the Digital Brain

Artificial intelligence, once the province

of science fiction, is now a vital

participant in the professional arena.

Investigate how AI is redefining work duties, from automating everyday activities to enhancing decision-making processes.

Discuss the importance of professionals adapting and gaining abilities that complement, rather than compete with, current technological improvements.

Emerging Technologies:

Pioneering the Next Wave

Beyond AI, a plethora of emergent

technologies, from blockchain to virtual

reality, fuel the digital revolution. Uncover how professionals may put themselves at the forefront of these advancements. Examine case studies of individuals who embraced emerging technology to carve out distinctive professional trajectories.

Challenges and Opportunities

Information Overload: Navigating the Sea of Data

In a world bombarded with information, professionals face the dilemma of choice. Explore ways for filtering, synthesizing, and extracting valuable insights from the deluge of data. Discuss the skills and conceptual frameworks that equip individuals to turn information overload into a strategic advantage.

Competition: Thriving in the Digital Arena

With the worldwide accessibility of digital platforms, professionals are no longer competing locally but on a global scale. Analyze the repercussions of this heightened rivalry and uncover the techniques to stand out amidst the digital throng. Case studies of successful digital workers will illustrate the roads to success.

Evolving Skill Requirements: The Digital Skillset

The competence expected by the digital world is in continual motion. Examine the talents that are increasingly necessary and how professionals may remain ahead of the curve. Dive into the notion of continual learning and the significance of

upskilling in ensuring career relevance.

Seizing Opportunities Amidst Challenges

Every obstacle in the digital realm

conceals an opportunity within its folds.

Explore the real-life experiences of

professionals who turned misfortune into

an advantage. Understand the mentality

and tactics that enable individuals to not

just weather hardships but emerge stronger

and more resilient.

As we traverse the complicated currents of the digital world, this chapter tries to present a panoramic picture of the trends impacting our professions and the dual nature of difficulties and possibilities that define the digital era. Let's go on this adventure to appreciate the subtleties of the digital career spectrum and create a route toward success.

CHAPTER 2

SIMPLIFY – STREAMLINING YOUR DIGITAL PRESENCE

Assessing Your Digital Footprint

In the broad digital realm, your online presence is your professional avatar, a dynamic depiction of your talents, accomplishments, and personality. As we enter into the process of streamlining your digital presence, the first critical step is to take stock of your existing footprint.

Crafting Your Digital Identity

Your digital identity is more than a collection of profiles; it's a narrative that recounts the tale of your professional life.

Walk readers through the process of self-assessment.

Encourage contemplation on the following:

Current Profiles: Analyze current social media profiles, professional networks, and personal websites. Evaluate the connection between these profiles and your

professional ambitions.

material Review: Examine the material

you've posted across platforms. Discuss

the value of having a consistent and

professional tone. Explore the influence of

content on your own brand.

Visibility: Assess how readily others can

discover you online. Discuss the

significance of visibility in the digital

domain and solutions for boosting

discoverability.

Understanding the impact

Explore the clear association between a well-crafted digital identity and employment chances. Discuss real-life instances of professionals who carefully modified their internet profiles to attract attention. Emphasize the relevance of authenticity in developing a digital identity that connects with both professional colleagues and potential employers.

Digital Decluttering

Techniques

The Digital Clutter Conundrum

In the age of knowledge, clutter can impede rather than help. Digital clutter is not only about files on your computer; it extends to emails, programs, and even internet contacts. This part educates readers with practical strategies to simplify their digital lives.

Email Management: Inbox Zen

The inbox is a hub of business communication, but it may easily become overwhelming. Provide ideas for clearing email inboxes, emphasizing the significance of classification, filters, and regular clean-up procedures. Share advice on obtaining 'inbox zero' and maintaining a simplified communication center.

App and tool evaluation

In the ever-expanding realm of digital tools, it's easy to acquire programs that may not fit your present needs. Guide

readers through a comprehensive

examination of their digital toolbox.

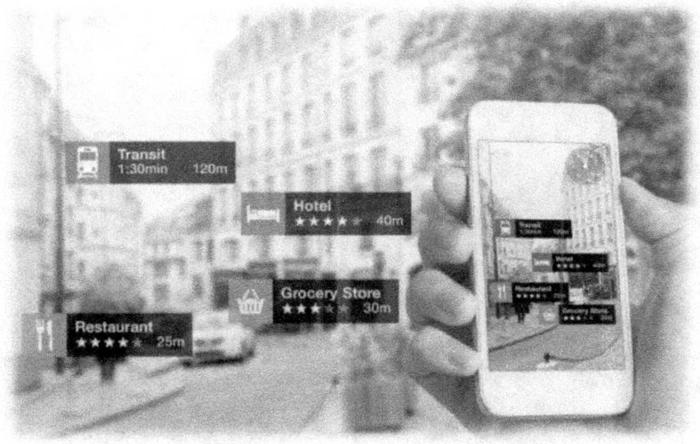

Discuss the criteria for determining which

applications and tools to keep, remove, or

investigate. Highlight the role of

efficiency and user friendliness in the

choosing process.

Social Media Sanity

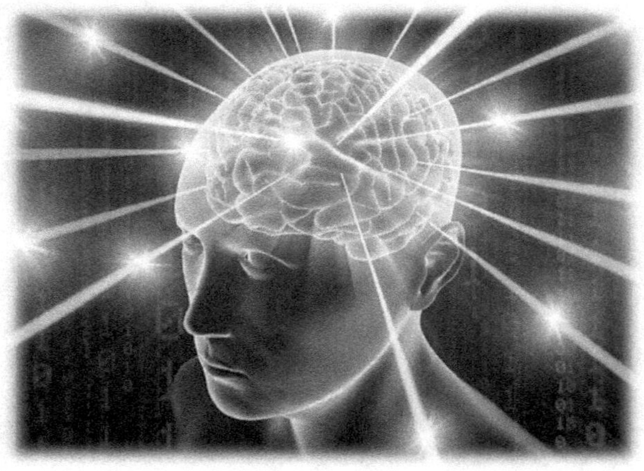

Social networking can be both a blessing

and a burden. Explore tactics for cleaning

social media profiles, managing friend

lists, and maximizing privacy settings.

Discuss the influence of social media on

professional reputation and ways to select

material that corresponds with career

goals.

Creating a Digital Organization System

Introduce readers to tools and approaches

for digital organizing. From cloud storage

options to task management applications, consider how these technologies may streamline work procedures and boost productivity.

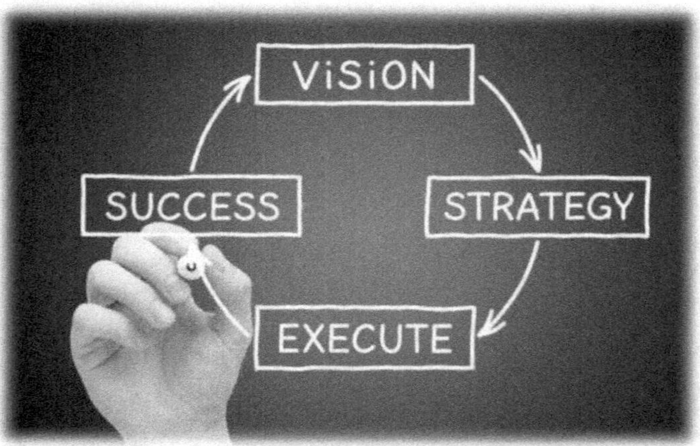

Provide insights on developing a tailored digital organization system that meets individual preferences and work patterns.

The Art of Digital Minimalism

Delve into the idea of digital minimalism, borrowing influence from minimalist principles. Discuss how adopting simplicity in the digital arena may lead to better attention, productivity, and general well-being.

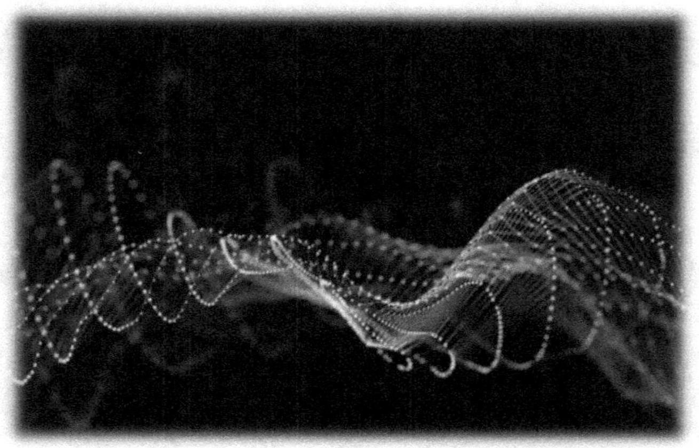

By the end of this chapter, readers will have not only examined their present digital presence but also received practical techniques to clear and streamline their online lives. The road toward a simpler digital presence is not only about decreasing noise; it's about developing a harmonic and impactful professional

identity in the digital symphony.

CHAPTER 3

ARRANGE – STRUCTURING YOUR DIGITAL CAREER

Building a Strong Personal

Brand

Unlocking the Essence of Personal Branding

In the digital arena, where attention spans are transient, a strong personal brand is your beacon of recognition. This section looks into the art of developing a compelling personal brand that connects with your career objectives.

Elements of a Powerful

Personal Brand

Break down the fundamental components

of a personal brand. Discuss the following

elements:

Brand Identity: Guide readers on how to define their own identity. Discuss the necessity of authenticity and connecting personal beliefs with the brand message.

Visual Cohesion: Explore the visual components of personal branding, including profile images, banners, and consistent color schemes. Share your thoughts on building a visually appealing and memorable brand aesthetic.

Brand Voice: Discuss the necessity of a consistent and genuine voice across multiple digital channels. Offer ideas on finding and maintaining a tone that matches one's professional self.

Value Proposition: Help readers establish their value proposition. Discuss ways to emphasize abilities, achievements, and unique selling qualities in a way that catches attention.

Aligning Brand with Career Goals

The harmony between personal brand and work objectives is crucial. Provide practical tasks for readers to connect their personal brand with their professional aspirations. Discuss case studies of individuals who effectively transformed their brand to open doors to new possibilities.

Consistency across Platforms

In the digital landscape, consistency is crucial. Guide readers on maintaining a unified brand message across numerous channels. Discuss techniques for changing brand messaging to meet the intricacies of multiple digital mediums while ensuring a consistent overarching theme.

Effective Networking in the

Digital Space

The Digital Networking Playground

networking has transcended physical

gatherings and boardrooms to become a

lively online pursuit. In this part, readers

will study tactics for effective networking

in the digital environment, employing

platforms and technologies to enhance

their professional contacts.

Strategic social media networking

Unpack the possibilities of social media

for business networking. Discuss

platform-specific techniques for LinkedIn,

Twitter, and other related networks.

Explore the usage of content sharing,

engaging with industry debates, and

networking with like-minded people.

Professional platforms and virtual events

Introduce readers to specific professional

sites meant for networking. Explore the

capabilities and advantages of platforms

like LinkedIn, highlighting the

significance of a polished profile and

active engagement in relevant groups.

Discuss the growth of virtual events and webinars as key networking tools. Offer insights about navigating virtual areas, developing important connections, and exploiting online events to extend one's professional circle.

Building and nurturing connections

Networking is not only about numbers but also quality. Guide readers on developing meaningful connections and fostering relationships. Discuss the art of individualized connection requests, efficient follow-ups, and the necessity of reciprocity in networking.

Online Mentorship and Collaboration

Explore the potential for mentoring and cooperation in the digital age. Discuss sites that encourage mentoring connections and ways to approach possible mentors online. Highlight the benefits of collaborative initiatives and how they may contribute to professional advancement.

Networking Etiquette in the Digital Age

Digital networking comes with its own set of etiquettes. Discuss the dos and don'ts of online networking, including good communication, courteous interaction, and avoiding common traps. By the conclusion of this chapter, readers will have the tools to not only establish a captivating personal brand but also traverse the digital networking world with confidence and strategic intent. The art of arranging a digital career path is about developing a framework that enhances one's professional identity and opens doors to significant relationships and possibilities.

CHAPTER 4

OPTIMIZE – MAXIMIZING DIGITAL OPPORTUNITIES

Leveraging Technology for Career Growth

The Tech Revolution in Career Development

In the ever-evolving digital world, technology isn't simply a tool; it's a catalyst for professional progress. This section shows the numerous ways in which professionals may employ technology to open new possibilities and move their careers ahead.

Digital tools for career advancement

Delve into the latest technologies and platforms that are revolutionizing the professional scene. Discuss categories

such as:

Project Management Tools: Explore systems that ease project collaboration and task management, boosting efficiency and productivity.

Communication Apps: Discuss the relevance of communication tools in facilitating cooperation, whether it's Slack for team communication or Zoom for virtual meetings.

Digital portfolio systems: Highlight the relevance of an online portfolio and provide systems that allow professionals to exhibit their work efficiently.

Networking applications: Explore applications created exclusively for professional networking, giving users the possibility to interact with industry colleagues, mentors, and possible collaborators.

Automation and efficiency

Discuss the use of automation in career optimization. Explore how professionals may utilize automation technologies to simplify repetitive work, allowing them to focus on more complicated and strategic parts of their employment. Provide instances of automation in various industries and explore the potential time and energy benefits.

Virtual collaboration and remote work

In the post-pandemic period, remote work and virtual collaboration have become fundamental components of the professional environment. Guide readers on harnessing technology to prosper in a remote work environment. Discuss virtual collaboration technologies, video conferencing best practices, and efficient distant communication tactics.

Strategic social media utilization

Social media isn't only a platform for personal interactions; it's a tremendous instrument for career success. Explore advanced tactics for leveraging sites like

LinkedIn, Twitter, and Instagram strategically.

Discuss the significance of social media in personal branding, networking, and staying current on industry developments.

Continuous Learning in the Digital Era

The Imperative of Lifelong Learning

In the digital world, continual learning isn't a luxury; it's a must. This section highlights the necessity of continual skill development and presents a plan for professionals to begin on a journey of lifetime learning.

Identifying skill gaps

Guide readers on reviewing their present skill sets and finding gaps that may limit professional growth. Discuss tactics for detecting growing industry demands and understanding the skills that are most relevant to their positions.

Online learning platforms

Explore the broad universe of online learning systems. Discuss major sites like Udemy, Coursera, and LinkedIn Learning, offering insights into the courses and certifications they provide. Highlight the flexibility and accessibility of online learning, enabling workers to upskill at their own pace.

Industry-Specific Resources

Different sectors have varied skill needs.

Offer help in discovering industry-specific

resources for continual learning. This

might include specialist forums, seminars,

and publications that cater to the specific

requirements of experts in a certain

industry.

Creating a Personalized Learning Plan:

Assist readers in building a tailored

learning plan. Discuss the value of

defining clear learning goals, constructing

a realistic plan, and combining skill

improvement with present work duties. Provide templates and examples to help readers structure their learning programs efficiently.

Networking for Learning Opportunities

Explore the relationship between networking and learning. Discuss how networking may lead to important learning opportunities, such as mentorship, information exchange, and joint initiatives. Highlight the symbiotic relationship between creating professional

relationships and learning new abilities.

Staying informed on industry trends

Discuss techniques for remaining updated

about industry developments. This

involves subscribing to relevant

periodicals, joining online forums, and

following thought leaders on social media.

Emphasize the significance of staying

ahead of industry trends in sustaining

professional relevance.

Overcoming learning challenges

Acknowledge the limitations of continual learning, such as time limits and information overload. Provide ways for overcoming these problems, including time management suggestions, targeted learning approaches, and the value of prioritizing learning as a professional investment. By the end of this chapter, readers will not only be armed with the newest tools and technology to boost their digital presence but will also grasp the important role of continual learning in keeping competitive and adaptable in the ever-evolving digital world.

Optimization in the digital career context isn't just about maximizing present chances; it's about developing a basis for continuous development and relevance.

CHAPTER 5

BALANCING ART – NAVIGATING WORK – LIFE HARMONY IN THE DIGITAL WORLD

Overcoming Digital Burn-out

The Perils of Constant Connectivity

The digital revolution, while offering incredible ease, has also ushered in the era of continual contact. This section digs into the issues of this 24/7 digital lifestyle and gives practical solutions to prevent and overcome digital burnout.

Understanding digital burnout

Define digital burnout and its symptoms. Discuss how the continual stream of emails, notifications, and virtual meetings might add to feelings of overload and tiredness. Utilize real-life examples and case studies to highlight the impact of digital burnout on professionals.

Setting Boundaries for Mental Well-Being

Guide readers on building appropriate boundaries in the digital sphere. Discuss the necessity of setting defined work hours, creating tech-free zones, and establishing guidelines for after-work interactions. Provide concrete advice for sustaining mental well-being, including mindfulness practices, stress reduction tactics, and the advantages of disconnecting.

Effective Time Management in a Digital World

Explore time management solutions geared to the digital work environment. Discuss the Pomodoro Technique, time blocking, and other approaches that help professionals retain concentration and productivity. Highlight the importance of prioritizing and work delegation in reducing the sense of being overwhelmed.

Promoting work-life integration

Challenge the established concept of work-life balance and promote the idea of work-life integration. Discuss how professionals may mix their personal and work lives in a way that increases overall well-being. Provide instances of successful work-life integration and how it contributes to a healthier and more fulfilled life.

Remote Work Success

The Rise of Remote

Work Remote employment has become a cornerstone of the modern professional environment. This section addresses the subtleties of remote work, giving insights, tools, and best practices to assure success in this growing work style.

Creating a productive home office

Guide readers on setting up an effective and ergonomic home office. Discuss the necessity of a separate workstation, sufficient lighting, and ergonomic furniture. Offer advice on eliminating distractions and establishing a suitable setting for concentrated work.

Effective Communication in a Virtual Environment

Explore the subtleties of virtual conversation. Discuss the limitations of expressing messages without a face-to-face connection and propose solutions for effective communication in virtual meetings. Address the necessity of clarity, attentive listening, and leveraging communication tools to bridge the gap in remote work situations.

Collaboration tools and techniques

Highlight the diversity of collaboration options accessible to distant teams. Discuss services like Slack, Microsoft Teams, and Zoom, sharing insights about their features and ideal use cases. Explore successful collaboration skills, including virtual brainstorming, project management, and file sharing.

Time Zone Management

For internationally distributed teams, coordinating multiple time zones is a vital

component of remote work. Offer
direction on arranging meetings, defining
standards for response times, and building
a feeling of inclusion for team members in
multiple locations.

Remote team building and employee engagement

Discuss techniques for developing a good
remote team culture. Explore virtual team-
building activities, online social events,
and strategies for promoting camaraderie

among team members who may never meet in person. Emphasize the significance of sustaining employee engagement and motivation in a remote work scenario.

Overcoming the Challenges of Remote Work

Acknowledge the problems involved with remote work, such as feelings of isolation, difficulty in team bonding, and potential misunderstanding. Provide realistic answers and coping methods for overcoming these problems so that professionals may thrive in a remote work environment.

By the conclusion of this chapter, readers will not only have a comprehensive awareness of the problems provided by continual connectivity and remote work but will also be armed with effective methods to maintain a good work-life balance and flourish in the digital work landscape. Balancing the demands of a digital job with personal well-being is not just a struggle; it's an art form, and this

chapter prepares professionals with the

tools to perfect it.

CHAPTER 6

FUTURE – PROOFING YOUR DIGITAL CAREER

Adapting to Change

Embracing the Inevitable: Change in the Digital Landscape

Change is the only constant in the digital universe. In this part, readers will study the inevitability of change and appreciate the fundamental need for flexibility and resilience in navigating a career through the ever-evolving world.

The Dynamics of Change in Digital Careers

Define the different sorts of change professionals may confront, from technology improvements to industry trends. Discuss how the pace of change has accelerated in the digital age and the influence this has on career paths. Utilize case studies and real-world examples to highlight how professionals have successfully managed substantial changes in their professions.

Staying Adaptable: A Skill Set for the Future

Guide readers on acquiring and strengthening adaptability as a key talent.

Discuss the mindset essential for embracing change, including a good attitude, curiosity, and a desire to learn. Offer practical activities and self-assessment tools to help professionals evaluate their adaptability and discover areas for growth.

Cultivating Resilience in the Face of Uncertainty

Explore the topic of resilience and its importance to career success. Provide insights on how professionals may foster resilience by forming a strong support network, developing coping skills, and reframing setbacks as chances for growth. Share examples of individuals who have overcome difficulties in their digital professions through perseverance.

Strategies for Navigating Career Transitions

Discuss frequent circumstances that may force job transfers, such as changes in industry demand, technological advances, or personal growth objectives. Offer practical ways for handling these

transitions smoothly, including upskilling,

networking, and seeking mentoring.

Emphasize the importance of a proactive

approach to career planning.

Emerging Trends and

Technologies

Anticipating Tomorrow: Exploring Upcoming Trends

Examine the notion of future-proofing by studying new trends and technology. Discuss the relevance of remaining updated about industry trends and how this information may be exploited to stay ahead in the digital job market.

Technology Trends Shaping the Future

Explore cutting-edge technologies that are predicted to shape the future digital world.

This might include artificial intelligence, blockchain, augmented reality, and other disruptive advancements. Break down difficult technology concepts into clearly understood language so that readers can realize the possible influence on their careers.

Preparing for the Jobs of Tomorrow

Discuss the development of employment roles in response to evolving technology. Provide insights on how professionals might match their skill sets with the jobs that will be in demand in the future.

Include case studies of people who have

effectively moved into positions that

evolved with the introduction of new

technology.

The Role of Continuous Learning in Future-Proofing

Reiterate the need for continual learning as

a strategy for future-proofing a digital

profession. Discuss how professionals

may remain current with evolving trends through online courses, workshops, and professional development opportunities. Provide a selected collection of resources and systems that enable continuing learning.

Building a personalized roadmap for future success

Guide readers in establishing a tailored path for their future success. Discuss the importance of defining objectives, identifying critical skills for development, and creating a plan for accomplishing professional milestones. Offer tools and frameworks that readers may use to build their own career plan.

Ethical Considerations in Emerging Technologies

Explore the ethical dimensions of new technology. Discuss the relevance of ethical issues in professional decision-making, especially in domains like artificial intelligence and data science.

Encourage professionals to match their

jobs with their principles and examine the

societal effect of their work.

Industry-Specific Trends and Predictions

Tailor the topic to individual sectors,

offering insights into the projected trends

and developments in each. Include

interviews with industry experts, case

studies of successful adjustments to industry transitions, and practical advice for professionals in many areas.

By the conclusion of this chapter, readers will not only grasp the inevitability of change in the digital world but will also be well-equipped with the skills, mentality, and knowledge needed to navigate and prosper in an ever-evolving digital job.

The future is unclear, but with the appropriate methods, professionals may approach it with confidence and anticipation, ready to welcome whatever challenges and possibilities come their way. Future-proofing is not just about surviving change; it's about prospering in it.

CHAPTER 7

DIGITAL LEADERSHIP AND INNOVATION

Defining digital leadership

Embracing the Digital Paradigm

The digital era has altered conventional leadership paradigms, giving rise to a new breed of digital leaders. Delve into the key ideas that separate digital leadership from its conventional counterparts. Explore how flexibility, technological aptitude, and strategic vision have become the cornerstone attributes of effective leadership in the digital era.

Traits of a Digital Leader

Identify and expound on the main talents and attributes that characterize a successful digital leader. From the capacity to traverse complicated technology environments to promoting creativity within teams, consider how these attributes help steer enterprises through the difficulties and possibilities of the digital era. Illustrate these themes using real-world instances of notable digital leaders.

Case Studies in Digital Leadership

Embark on a journey via case studies that show the influence of digital leadership on organizational performance. Explore how digital leaders have organized dramatic shifts, handled challenges, and established cultures of continuous improvement. These stories give real-life instances of how successful digital leadership may catapult enterprises to unimaginable heights.

Fostering Innovation in the Digital Workspace

The Essence of Innovation

Examine the critical role innovation plays

in influencing the success of digital

efforts. Define innovation in the context of

the digital workspace and explore why it's vital for firms looking for relevance and sustainability. Illustrate how innovation extends beyond technological developments to embrace numerous aspects of business culture and procedures.

Strategies for a Culture of Innovation

Delve into practical ways for building a culture of creativity within digital teams. Explore approaches for ideation, experimentation, and collaboration that allow team members to participate in the innovation process. Highlight the value of diversity, open communication, and a development mentality in building an atmosphere where new ideas may bloom.

Showcasing Innovation and Success

Present case studies of firms that have effectively adopted a culture of continuous innovation. These examples highlight how creative thinking has turned into actual business benefits, from improved goods and services to increased consumer experiences. By reviewing these success stories, readers receive insights into the

actual application of new approaches.

Digital Ethics and

Responsibility

Navigating the Ethical Landscape of Digital Careers

Ethical Considerations in a Digital World Examine the ethical problems that professionals experience in the digital sphere. Discuss problems such as data privacy, cybersecurity, and the ethical use of technology. Offer insights on the complexity of ethical decision-making in the workplace, including the ever-evolving landscape of digital jobs.

The Human Element in Digital Ethics

Explore the influence of technology on human interactions and ethical dilemmas. Discuss how digital workers may strike the tricky balance between embracing technology for productivity and upholding ethical standards. Illustrate these themes using real-world examples that emphasize the ethical challenges inherent in digital jobs.

Guidance for Ethical Decision-Making

Provide practical help on making ethical judgments in the fast-paced and complicated world of digital jobs. Discuss concepts and ways that professionals might apply to ensure their behaviors fit with ethical norms. Empower readers with the tools to navigate the ethical terrain, promoting a sense of duty and integrity.

Social Responsibility in Digital Professions

The Role of Digital Professionals in Society

Examine the notion of social responsibility in the context of digital professions.

Discuss how professionals may contribute to social well-being through their employment, outside the limitations of company aims. Explore opportunities for solving social challenges, encouraging diversity and inclusion, and harnessing technology for beneficial social effects.

Diversity and Inclusion in Digital Workplaces

Discuss the relevance of diversity and inclusion in digital workplaces. Explore how embracing diversity adds to innovation and creativity within organizations. Showcase efforts and practices that digital workers and companies may implement to promote inclusive workplaces, encouraging a sense of belonging and fair opportunity.

Technology for social good

Illustrate how technology can be a force for societal good. Showcase examples of individuals and groups embracing digital tools to address major social challenges, from healthcare and education to environmental sustainability.

By spotlighting these activities, we urge readers to examine the larger influence of their work in the digital environment. By covering the elements of digital leadership, innovation, ethics, and social responsibility, this chapter lays the framework for readers to manage the intricacies of the ever-evolving digital ecosystem.

As professionals seek to lead and innovate ethically, they become architects of good change, determining the future of digital careers.

CHAPTER 8

MASTERING DIGITAL COMMUNICATION

Crafting a Digital

Communication Plan

The importance of clear communication

Discuss why clear and succinct communication is crucial in the digital era. Explore how information overload may lead to misconceptions and inefficiencies, underscoring the necessity for a well-thought-out communication plan. Provide examples of communication failures and their effects to show the necessity of good digital communication.

Developing your communication strategy

Guide readers through the process of

building a complete digital communication

plan. Break down the pieces of a

successful strategy, including audience

study, message creation, and platform

selection. Offer practical suggestions,

templates, and examples to equip

professionals to design communication

strategies specific to their individual aims

and audiences.

Tools and Technologies for Digital Communication

Explore the plethora of tools and technology available for efficient digital communication. Discuss communication platforms, project management tools, and collaborative software that can expedite communication procedures. Highlight the benefits and possible obstacles connected with these technologies, ensuring readers can make educated judgments about integrating them into their communication plans.

Building a Personal Brand via Digital Communication

The Power of Personal Branding

Examine how professionals may utilize digital communication to establish and strengthen their personal brand. Discuss the significance of narrative, content generation, and thought leadership in developing a successful online presence. Provide instances of individuals who have effectively curated their personal brand through digital media, highlighting the influence of purposeful and planned communication.

Content creation for digital platforms

Explore successful content development tactics for digital platforms. Discuss the forms of material that resonate with viewers, such as blog articles, videos, and social media updates. Provide practical direction on developing interesting and shareable content, emphasizing the value of authenticity and consistency in building a compelling personal brand.

Measuring Personal Brand Impact

Guide readers in assessing the influence of their personal brand through digital communication. Discuss essential metrics, analytics tools, and feedback methods that professionals may use to analyze the efficacy of their communication efforts. Encourage constant modification and adaptation based on the insights received from measuring the personal brand effect.

Navigating Digital Challenges

Overcoming Digital Challenges in Your Career

Information overload and digital burnout

Discuss the frequency of information

overload and digital burnout in current digital employment. Explore the influence of continual connectedness on mental well-being and professional happiness. Provide ways for managing information overload, creating boundaries, and minimizing digital burnout, ensuring professionals can flourish in the digital era.

Imposter Syndrome in the Digital Realm

Examine the problem of impostor syndrome in digital jobs. Discuss why people in digital positions may suffer from impostor syndrome and suggest practical techniques for overcoming it. Share personal tales and case studies of individuals who have successfully navigated impostor syndrome, promoting resilience and confidence in readers.

Continuous learning and adaptation

Emphasize the necessity of ongoing learning and adaptability in the face of digital challenges. Discuss the fast rate of change in digital sectors and how professionals may stay relevant by obtaining new skills and expertise. Provide tools, online courses, and professional development opportunities to enable continuing learning and adaptability.

Networking and Collaborating in a Digital World

Strategic digital networking

Explore sophisticated techniques for digital networking. Discuss how professionals should strategically employ digital platforms to develop meaningful professional relationships. Provide insights into discovering and engaging with significant influencers, peers, and mentors in the digital arena. Share the success stories of individuals who have boosted their careers through savvy internet networking.

Collaborating Effectively in the Digital Space

Discuss the subtleties of effective collaboration in a digital environment. Explore virtual collaboration tools, project management systems, and communication channels that facilitate digital cooperation. Provide case studies of effective digital cooperation, highlighting best practices and lessons learned. Empower professionals to navigate and flourish in collaborative digital contexts.

Building and Maintaining a Digital Network

Guide readers in developing and sustaining a healthy digital network. Discuss the ideas of reciprocity, trust-building, and value exchange in digital networking. Provide practical suggestions for maintaining connections with network connections, fostering relationships, and exploiting the network for professional growth. Illustrate the long-term benefits of a well-maintained digital professional network.

By learning effective digital communication tactics and overcoming the hurdles inherent in digital jobs, workers may position themselves for success in the ever-evolving digital ecosystem. This chapter prepares readers with the information and techniques needed to communicate strategically, overcome problems, and prosper in the changing world of digital work.

CONCLUSION

Summarize Key Takeaways

Simplification, Arrangement, and Optimization:

A Recap In this closing chapter, let's explore the key ideas of simplicity, arrangement, and optimization that have served as the guiding beacons throughout our investigation of "The Base Strategy: Simplify, Arrange, and Optimize Your Digital Career."

1. Simplify

Recall the importance of simplifying your internet presence and clearing excessive digital noise. Understand how a focused and consistent online persona may boost your professional image and open doors to new prospects.

2. Arrange

Reflect on the necessity of building your digital career through effective personal branding and smart networking. Explore the complexities of developing a personal brand that corresponds with your goals, and discover the skill of exploiting digital platforms for meaningful professional relationships.

3. *Optimize*

Revisit the techniques for exploiting digital possibilities, embracing technology for professional success, and committing to ongoing learning. Understand how staying ahead of industry trends and responding to change may position you as a digital leader in your sector.

Key Lessons from Each Chapter

Chapter 1: The Landscape of the Digital Career

Explore the growing trends impacting the digital world, recognizing both difficulties and possibilities. Understand the importance of remaining educated about industry trends and adjusting to the changing needs of the digital world.

Chapter 2: Simplify: Streamlining Your Digital Presence

Learn to examine your digital footprint and adopt digital decluttering practices. Discover tools and ways to streamline your online presence, ensuring that it corresponds with your professional goals.

Chapter 3: Arrange: Structuring Your Digital Career

Delve into the area of personal branding and successful networking in the digital environment. Understand how to establish a strong personal brand and harness digital channels for smart networking.

Chapter 4: Optimize: Maximizing Digital Opportunities
Explore the significance of technology in professional progression and the need for constant learning. Learn how to harness digital tools, platforms, and trends to maximize your digital career for success.

Chapter 5: Balancing Act: Navigating Work-Life Harmony in the Digital World
Address the issues of persistent connectivity and distant work. Discover ways to minimize digital burnout and achieve success while maintaining a good work-life balance.
Chapter 6: Future-Proofing Your Digital Career
Understand the inevitability of change in the digital ecosystem and examine

upcoming trends and technology. Learn to adapt to change and position yourself for success in an ever-evolving digital world.

Chapter 7: Digital Leadership and Innovation

Define digital leadership and investigate the role of innovation in the digital workspace. Discuss digital ethics and social responsibility, highlighting the relevance of ethical decision-making in the digital domain.

Chapter 8: Mastering Digital Communication

Master efficient digital communication tactics and handle hurdles in the digital realm. Learn to develop a personal brand through digital communication and overcome digital hurdles in your work.

Encouragement for the Digital

Journey Ahead:

A Proactive and Positive Approach As you

begin your digitally optimized career,

remember that the path is a constant

adventure packed with chances for

development and adaptability. Embrace a proactive and optimistic approach, viewing setbacks as stepping stones to achievement. Fostering empowerment and confidence You have obtained a full arsenal for managing the growing digital world. Use this information to empower yourself, confident in your capacity to not just survive but thrive in the digital age. Your career is a dynamic canvas, and you are the artist defining its tale. The ever-adapting digital landscape

The digital world will continue to develop, providing new difficulties and great possibilities. Keep interested, keep educated, and stay adaptive. Your dedication to lifelong learning and digital excellence will be the spark for sustainable success.

In conclusion, "The Base Strategy: Simplify, Arrange, and Optimize Your Digital Career" is not simply a book; it's a guide for your digital journey. Apply the ideas, modify the techniques, and go ahead with confidence. Your digitally optimized career awaits thrive in the digital age!